Tyneside: Past and

A journey through time &

by

Geoff Phillips

Published by G P Electronic Services
87 Willowtree Avenue
Durham
DH1 1DZ
Tel: 091 384 9707

First published 1993

ISBN 0 9522480 0 X

Front cover design, interior design and graphics by Geoff Phillips.

Present day photographs by Craig Oliphant.

Printed by:
Smith Print Group Limited, Sutherland House, South Shore Road, Gateshead. Tel: 091 490 1001

CONTENTS

Tyneside: Past and Present

Introduction

This book has been compiled as a sequel to "Newcastle: Past and Present" which has enjoyed immense popularity over the last three years. Part of the success of Newcastle: Past and Present was the presentation of photographs of scenes of Newcastle as they were at the turn of the century and modern photographs taken from the same vantage points. In many cases there are buildings or points of reference that have remained intact which convince the doubting reader that the two photographs are indeed of the same view. Sometimes the links between the old and new photographs are obvious, but in many cases they are hard to find and searching for the links adds to the enjoyment of Tyneside: Past and Present.

Tyneside: Past and Present gives the reader a wider view of Geordieland by including scenes of the suburbs of Newcastle and Tyneside towns such as Tynemouth, Cullercoats and Whitley Bay.

This book is based on the Jack Phillips Collection of old photographs of the north-east of England; a collection which the author inherited from his late father. Jack was a keen amateur historian and started collecting old photographs, sketches and historical notes in the 1940's. He liaised closely with Newcastle Central Library and was often called upon to give talks about the history of Newcastle and presentations of his collection. He enjoyed publicity and from time to time the Evening Chronicle newspaper included an article about Jack's collection.

In Jack's younger days, his passion was music. He played the Hawaiian guitar in his own band and is shown in the centre of the photograph on the next page, supplying the music for a dance at the Coxlodge CWS on 10 April 1948. The pianist is Horsley Hall who is also a keen historian, specialising in Tyneside's past. The line-up is Aaron Robertson, Joe Hanley, Stan Wood, Jack Phillips and Horsley Hall.

The Jack Phillips Hawaiian Band at Coxlodge CWS hall in 1948

A Journey Through Time and Tyneside

Pay the toll and travel through the time tunnel to Tyneside's past. The photographs in this book have been arranged in sequence to form a journey through Tyneside as it used to be and as it is now. The first part of the journey is around the streets of Newcastle upon Tyne and is best conducted on foot. If the traveller is using private transport it is suggested that one of the car parks on the Quayside underneath the Tyne Bridge is used. This area should be avoided on a Sunday from 10am till 2 pm as this is the day of the Quayside's traditional open air market. On a Sunday parking on the streets of Newcastle is much easier (but not free of charge). The second part of the journey is best made by car and includes suburbs and villages in north-east Tyneside. There are plenty of stops for refreshment at inns and taverns along the way (non-alcoholic drinks for the driver please).

Journey Around the Streets of Newcastle.

The first view is of the High Level Bridge taken from the Gateshead banks of the Tyne. Walk across the Swing Bridge from Newcastle's Quayside and turn right along Pipewell Gate. Walk past the Bretts Oils depot and you will come to a grassed area overlooking the Tyne. This is the closest you may get to view No1 without paddling into the Tyne. It was Robert Stephenson who built the High Level Bridge which was designed to carry road vehicles on the lower level and railway trains on the top level. The cast iron and masonry bridge was completed in 1849 and is still in service today although Stephenson would never have guessed that a century and a half later it would be carrying double-decker buses, lorries, cars and inter-city diesel trains simultaneously.

Walk back across the Swing Bridge and turn right when you will come to Sandhill and view No2. This view shows the 16-17th century timber-framed merchants' houses one of which belonged to Auburn Surtees, a rich banker in the late 18th century. Mr Surtees' daughter, Bessie, fell in love with John Scott and they wanted to marry. Bessie's father objected to the marriage because John had not completed his education and was considered too young. On 18 November, 1772, John and Bessie eloped and were married in Scotland.

The impressive structure of the Tyne Bridge above was built by Dorman Long & Co of Middlesborough in 1928. Later the same company built the Sydney Harbour Bridge to a similar design.

Walk towards the River Tyne and continue along the Quayside in an easterly direction until you come to the new law courts. This is where the old view No3 was taken. Retrace your steps and turn right along Broad Chare and stop for a while to observe the Trinity Maritime Centre and Trinity House. Chares were narrow lanes which ran between main roads and were usually only wide enough for two people to walk past each other. Broad Chare was so named as it was enough for a horse and cart to pass along. Continue up the hill towards the Church of All Saints and walk through the underpass system to the Joicey Museum which occupies the building of what used to be the Holy Jesus hospital founded by the Corporation in 1681. This museum of Newcastle's social history contains plans, costumes, furniture, paintings and period interiors. Entry to the museum is free.

After leaving the museum turn right and pass through the subway system again following the signs for Swan House. Climb the stairs to see view No4, a replica of part of the interior of Grainger's Royal Arcade of 1831. Walk though the arcade and when you are outdoors again you will see a memorial to Joseph W. Swan, the Tyneside inventor of the electric light bulb.

Take the elevated walkway to the New Science Park near Manors station, enter the park's courtyard and watch out for Manors British Rail station. This used to be New Bridge Street Station and is where photograph No5 was taken; the first electric train to run on the North-East Coast Line. The Tyneside Metro system now runs underground here and access to the station is north of the Science Park.

Re-join the elevated walkway system and follow the signs to Mosely Street. Walk west along Mosely Street and before continuing into Collingwood Street take time to survey the beautiful St Nicholas' Cathedral. Continue along Collingwood Street and stand underneath the multi-storey office block and look east to see view No6, Collingwood Street. Here you will see Stephenson's Monument in memory of George Stephenson who was famous for the building of the Stockton to Darlington railway. His son Robert Stephenson was also noted for his engineering achievements.

View No7 may also be seen here at the corner of Westgate Road and Neville Street. The single gatepost is all that remains of the Virgin Mary Hospital which became the premises for the Royal Grammar School.

Find the narrow lane called Pudding Chare and walk north to see views No8 and No9. This area was noted for being the centre of the printing trade and, indeed, the offices and printing works of the Newcastle Chronicle and Journal newspapers are situated here.

Pudding Chare emerges at the Bigg Market which used to be where farmers would bring a variety of barley called Bigg to be sold. Today the Bigg Market is better known by young Tynesiders as a centre for clubs, pubs, and restaurants where many a reveller has fallen foul of the law for rowdy behaviour. Continue through the Bigg Market along a street called High Bridge. This street was named after a bridge over the Lort Burn; a stream which ran down the length of where Grey Street now stands. Turn left into Grey Street and walk uphill passing the Theatre Royal on your right. On reaching Grey's Monument, look south down Grey Street to see view No 10 and marvel at the elegance of this fine street constructed by Grainger in 1836.

Walk south down Grainger Street, named after the man himself, and turn right into Nelson Street just opposite the Central Arcade. Walk along Nelson Street and look up to read the names of the buildings sculptured into the stone walls. At the top of Nelson Street turn around to see view No11.

Head back along Grainger Street to Grey's Monument and walk east along Blackett Street. Here you will see view No12 Northumberland Street. Views a) and b) were both probably taken from the top deck of a tram. Northumberland Street is now pedestrianised which makes for relatively easy progress north to see views No13 and No14. Northumberland Street is shoppers paradise with large department stores, clothes and shoe shops along with a selection of restaurants and fast food establishments.

Continue north to the Haymarket to see views No15 and No16. The angel on the stone pillar in the Haymarket is a memorial to the men who died in the Boer War in South Africa. View No16 is actually taken from a spot known as Barras Bridge which is thought to be a corruption of bars or barriers bridge being a bridge near the barriers of the town. Quite close to the Hancock Museum is a door which gives access to the Victoria Tunnel which passes underneath Newcastle and was used to transport coal from Spital Tongues to the Quayside. The tunnel was used as an air raid shelter during the second world war.

Cross the road at the pedestrian crossing opposite St Thomas' Church and head north-west along Claremont Road. The Hancock Museum is on the right and the University of Newcastle upon Tyne is on the left. After a hundred yards or so you will come to the entrance of the Exhibition Park and view No17. The exhibition was opened by the Prince of Wales on May 12, 1929 and attracted over 4 million visitors. Impressive structures called "Palaces" were erected which housed exhibits of Science, engineering, agriculture and art. The exhibition was built to demonstrate to the rest of the nation what the North-East could offer in terms of industrial know-how, skills and expertise. The exhibition also featured a mile-long roller-coaster called the Himalayan Railway and an African mud-hut village where 100 Senegalese lived and shivered in the cold Tyneside climate. Only a fraction of the 1929 park remains and the Palace of Arts is the only main structure still standing which overlooks a boating lake.

After visiting the park, re-trace your steps to the Haymarket and travel south along Percy Street alongside the bus station. View No18 is the impressive brick structure known as the Newcastle Breweries Building. To the left of this are Bruce's Buildings which were built on the site of Bruce's Academy, founded by John Bruce in 1806. View No19 looks north towards the Haymarket again and shows the immense changes which have taken place since the early photograph.

Cross Percy Street and continue south under the Eldon Gardens bridge and when you are opposite Leazes Lane notice that the wall on the building on the corner seems to slope outover in a precarious manner. This shows that the old photograph of the Morpeth Castle pub (No20) is in fact the same building.

Continue south along Percy Street and turn right into Gallowgate. This road used to lead to the town gallows which were situated on the town moor. Aptly, the Jailer's house was situated close to the junction of Percy Street and Gallowgate but was known by many Geordie's as Bourgognes public house (view No21) Views No22 and No23 may be seen on Gallowgate itself.

The walk around Newcastle is now complete and the next section of the journey takes us east to the suburb of Byker.

The Journey Around Tyneside Towns, Villages, and Suburbs.
Assuming your transport is parked on the Quayside, head east past the new law courts and then turn left to climb the bank to travel east on City Road. As you climb the bank notice the distinctive architecture of Sallyport tower which was one of the towers around the City Wall. Continue along City Road, past the Tyne-Tees Television Studios and when the road starts to go downhill, take the next left and descend to cross the Ouseburn, a tributary of the River Tyne. Notice Byker Bridge on the left as you climb Byker Bank. At the top of the bank you will see view No24, where the Byker Tavern used to stand. The Byker Wall housing complex is on the right and continues east parallel to Shields Road. Carry on up Shields Road and at the top of the road you will see view No25 The Blue Bell pub. Just before the Blue Bell turn left into Algernon Road and park in the car park there. The next few views are best seen by foot. View No26, Byker Square may be seen by walking east and crossing Shields Road opposite the petrol filling station. Walk north along Shields Road past St Mark's Church and cross the road again to see view No27. North View School was situated on Brough Street which is now difficult to find in the new Byker housing complex. The easiest route is to walk down Chillingham Road and turn left before the railway bridge. Walk along parallel to the railway and you will come to Northfields House on the left. This senior citizen's sheltered accommodation complex was built on the site of North View School. View No28 may be seen by turning left after Northfields House. This is Brough Street. There used to be a sweet shop on the corner which was popular with schoolchildren. Find your way back onto Shields Road and walk east downhill towards the Byker Car Sheds where you will see view No29. View No30 was taken inside the depot.

Return to your transport and drive along Chillingham Road to see view No 31 where Chillingham Road crosses the Coast Road. In the 1960's the Coast Road was widened to almost motorway standard with motorway style intersections built at each junction with existing roads.

Cross the Coast Road after which Chillingham Road leads to Benton Road. View No 32 is at Four Lane Ends where Benton Road meets Benton Lane, Front Street and Benton Park Road. Turn right here along Front Street and notice the very old pubs along this route (The Sun, Black Bull and The Ship) which were probably all present at the time of view No32a.

At the second set of traffic lights turn left and head towards Forest Hall. The road passes through a tree-lined cutting near Benton Station which is where the electric train coast line used to terminate before it was extended to Monkseaton. The station is now part of the Tyneside Metro system. In Victorian times it was very fashionable to live in this part of Newcastle and many of the houses you will see here are in the grand Victorian mansion style.

Continue towards Forest Hall and drive over the flyover and turn left into the old village area to see view No33. Forest Hall was actually named after a hall which was built in 1625 for Richard Wilson. Sadly the hall no longer exists.

View No34, The Clousden Hill pub (Tut 'n' Shive) may be seen by returning to the main part of Station Road heading east. The road turns sharp left, past what used to be the Ritz cinema and brings you out at Great Lime Road.

Turn right here and head east along Great Lime Road. The road joins the Old Coast Road or Whitley Road at Benton Square. Travel east on the Whitley Road and before you reach the large round-a-bout intersection notice the very old pub The Holystone on the left. At the round-a-bout follow the signs to West Allotment. This is the A191 and actually bypasses New York however you can see view No35, The Wheatsheaf Inn from the main road. The Stephenson railway museum is quite near and worth a visit.

Head back the way you came along the A191 and turn right at the signs to Shiremoor. After Shiremoor turn right at the traffic lights onto Earsdon Road (A186) and before you reach the round-a-bout turn left and be transported back in time in the lovely village of Earsdon. here you will see view No 36, The Cannon Inn.

At the round-a-bout take the A192 to Seaton Deleval but take an immediate right turn onto the B1325 to see view No37, The Bee Hive Inn. This is a fascinating pub which dates back 250 years. For many years it had no mains electricity and the pints of beer were drawn straight from the wooden barrels in a walk-in ground-level beer storage area.

Continue along the B1325 to the village of Old Hartley (view No38). Coal was worked in this area as early as the 13th century. In the 18th Century this area was famous for its bottle works. Outside the Deleval Arms pub you will see a large stone called the Hartley Blue Stone. A famous north-east strongman called Willie Carr who was born in Hartley's old engine house, was able to lift this stone above his head. Many men tried to lift the stone and many men failed.

At the round-a-bout, head south towards Whitley Bay on the A193 to view No39, St Mary's Island. This is a very photogenic island which is well worth seeing. At low tide you may walk across the causeway and visit the museum which is housed in the lighthouse. The area is also popular with naturalists.

Head towards Whitley Bay and follow the A193 through the town to see views No40 and No41. Continue on the A193 on the Marden Road and turn left at Marden Avenue to Cullercoats Metro Station to see view No42. Head towards the coast and turn right and if time permits, park and walk along the wonderful Tynemouth Long Sands. View No43 may be seen at Tynemouth high street called Front Street.

Leave Tynemouth on the A193 and turn right at the A192, Preston Road. View No44 is tucked away, near the Tynemouth Swimming Pool at the junction of the A192 and the A1058. Continue along the A1058, which becomes a 3 lane motorway style road; the Coast Road. View No45 may be seen before you pass under the railway bridge soon after the A186 intersection.

The Coast Road returns you Newcastle and in order to see view No46 you must drive out of the city west on the A69. The view is on the West Road at Denton Burn.

The final view, A Tram at Lemington may be seen by turning left at the A69's intersection with Union Hall Road and passing through the village to join the A6085.

1. (a) High Level Bridge & Stone Tyne Bridge   c1865

This photograph shows Newcastle from the Gateshead banks of the Tyne in about 1865. The High Level Bridge was opened in 1849 and allowed the rail link from London to be extended north to Scotland. The old stone bridge was replaced by the Swing Bridge in 1876. The very first bridge across the Tyne at Newcastle was built by the Romans in AD120; the Bridge of Aelius took its name from the family name of the Emperor Hadrian who also gave his name to the famous wall.

(b) 1993

The author would like to thank Mr Brett of Bretts Oils for allowing us to take the 1993 view from their premises in Gateshead. The 1993 view shows the distinctive steel arch of the Tyne Bridge built in 1928.

2. (a) Sandhill 1926

This view shown the 16-17th century timber-framed merchants' houses one of which was Auburn Surtees House; a wealthy Newcastle banker. In 1776, Mr Surtees' daughter Bessie eloped with John Scott, the son of a coal merchant, as Bessie's father would not allow her to marry John as he considered him to be too young.

(b) Title

John Scott later became a successful barrister and entered Parliament. In 1788 he was made solicitor general and was knighted. In 1801 he became Lord Chancellor a position he kept almost continuously for 26 years.

3.(a) Quayside 1890

This view shows two of the many public houses in Newcastle in the late 1800's; The Scotch Arms and The Bridge Inn.

(b) New Law Courts 1993

The scene is now dominated by the prestigious new law courts completed in 1990.

4.(a) The Royal Arcade

Built by Grainger in 1832, the Royal Arcade was one of the first shopping "malls" long before Eldon Square or the Metro Centre. Victorian gentlemen and their ladies would stroll down the concourse of elegant shops in one of the most fashionable shopping thoroughfares. Its popularity was short lived however as retailers moved to other parts of the city. In 1966 the arcade was demolished to make way for a traffic intersection with the Central Motorway East.

(b) Royal Arcade facsimile in Swan House

The Arcade was dismantled stone by stone with a plan to rebuild it elsewhere. The re-building never took place but as a compromise, a facsimile of the arcade concourse was manufactured from wood and plaster on the ground floor of a massive office block built above the traffic intersection.

5.(a) First Electric Train 1904

On March 29th 1904 at 12:50 pm the first electric train of a new service left New Bridge Street Station (now Manors) for Benton full of excited passengers. It was the first electrified suburban train service in Britain and took only 11 minutes to travel the 5 miles including two stops at intermediate stations. This was a saving of 4 minutes on the steam train time. In June 1904 the service was extended from Benton to Monkseaton.

(b) Metro Train 1993

The last electric train ran on the line 63 years later on June 17th 1967 after which diesel trains took over. Ironically, soon after all the electric rails had been torn up, negotiations between the PTA and British Rail resulted in proposals for a new electrified rapid transit system using largely the same routes. Fourteen years later the Tyneside Metro system was opened. This view shows one of the Metro trains pulling into Manors Metro station which is now underground

6.(a) Collingwood Street. Blaydon Races Procession 1901

Collingwood Street is mentioned in the Geordie song "The Blaydon Races" and it is believed that this photograph shows the Blaydon Races procession in 1901. On the left building work on the new Barclays Bank is underway.

(b) 1848

This is an earlier shot of the same view. Westgate Road has not been extended yet. This photograph must have been one of the very first taken of Newcastle upon Tyne.

(c) 1990

Westgate Road now continues on down to St Nicholas Street and the entrance to the High Level Bridge.

7.(a) Westgate Road

This photograph was taken from almost the same spot as the previous shot but we are now facing south towards Neville Street. On the corner of the Express Hotel is one of the gateposts of the Royal Grammar School which was first established in the reign of Henry VIII by Alderman Thomas Horsley. The school actually occupied what was originally the Virgin Mary Hospital and was eventually demolished in 1844.

(b) 1993

The gatepost still remains; the Royal Grammar School is now in Eskdale Terrace in Jesmond. The Express Hotel was demolished in 1971 and has been replaced with an enormous office block but just around the other side of the block is a bar called the Express.

8. (a) Pudding Chare 1924

Pudding Chare is a narrow street which runs from Collingwood Street to the Bigg Market. This view shows the Lord Collingwood public house which was established in 1855. The area was and still is a centre for the printing industry.

(b) 1990

The Newcastle Chronicle offices and printing works adjoin Pudding Chare.

9. (a) Pudding Chare 2   c1924

This is a view of Pudding Chare looking south.

(b) 1991

The tall buildings on the left are the offices of the Newcastle Chronicle and Journal newspapers. To the left, out of view is the Printer's Pie public house.

10.(a) Grey Street, 1920

This is a view of one Newcastle's most elegant streets. The Newcastle Picture House is seen on the left and the Theatre Royal's frontage can be seen jutting out, three blocks further south.

(b) 1993

Little has changed to the architecture in this street since it was built in 1836. It was named after the Right Hon. Charles, Earl Grey K.G. who was noted for his work in connection with the Reform Bill of 1832.

11. (a) Nelson Street

Built by Grainger in a similar style to Grainger Street, Nelson Street connects Clayton Street to Grainger Street. The Gaiety Theatre is seen in the centre of the photograph. The Gaiety was originally called the Lecture Room and in 1861 Charles Dickens gave readings there from David Copperfield and Nicholas Nickleby. For many years it was a music hall and eventually as a cinema until it was closed as a fire risk in 1949.

(b) 1993

Little has changed to the architecture of this fine street.

12.(a) Northumberland Street 1935

Northumberland Street has always been very popular with shoppers as this view confirms. The photograph was taken at the time of the coronation of George VI. Flags are flying on the roof of Fenwicks department store as pedestrians risk life and limb picking their way through the traffic.

(b) 1940's

(c) 1993

The shop which used to be Amos Atkinson's boot and shoe shop is still standing on the right but the new Monument Mall now occupies the corner site of Blackett Street and Northumberland Street on the left of the picture.

13.(a) Northumberland Street 2 c1900

This view is slightly further north and shows Amos Atkinson's boot and shoe shop in more detail. The Star Hotel is shown in the centre of the photograph and to the left are Nuttall contractors carrying out some repairs to the road.

(b) 1990

The shoe shop was still called Amos Atkinsons up until about 1991 when it changed its name to The Suit Co.

14. (a) Fenwick's Department Store 1885

Victorian Newcastle was a time of great commercial growth with the opening of department stores such as Bainbridges and Fenwicks. This was Fenwick's first store on Northumberland Street.

(b) Fenwick's Department Store 1993

This fine building was erected in 1923 and Fenwick's store is still as popular as ever for good quality merchandise.

15.(a) Haymarket, looking south c1910

The South African War Memorial, built in 1906 dominates the view. This was a popular meeting place as public transport from some of the suburbs of Newcastle terminated here.

(b) 1993

The Haymarket is still a focus of public transport having a Tyneside Metro underground station and a bus station within a few yards of each other.

16.(a) Hancock Museum, Great North Road c1900

The Hancock Museum of Natural History was opened in 1884. The view shows the Great North Road which leads out of Newcastle upon Tyne, past the Town Moor where the annual fair called the Hoppings is held.

(b) 1993

The Hancock Museum is still standing and exhibits many of the original works of famous taxidermists. The Great North Road was victim of the "spaghetti-junction" phenomenon.

17.(a) North East Coast Exhibition 1929

The exhibition was opened by the Prince of Wales on May 12 and attracted over 4 million visitors. Impressive structures called "Palaces" were erected which housed exhibits of Science, engineering, agriculture and art. The exhibition was built to demonstrate to the rest of the nation what the North-East could offer in terms of industrial know-how, skills and expertise.

(b) Exhibition Park 1993

The only Palace remaining is the Palace of Arts which is now a museum of military transport. The Central Motorway system now bisects the park and pedestrians must now use an underpass to reach the Palace of Arts.

18.(a) Percy Street 1870

This photograph is in unusually good condition considering it was taken over 120 years ago. The Haymarket public house can be seen at the extreme right of the picture and Bruce's Buildings are at the extreme left. The Bruce's Buildings stand on the site of Bruce's Academy which was founded by John Bruce in 1806.

(b) 1993

Mr Lumsden's store was replaced by this fine building in 1900 being the Newcastle Breweries Building which was their main office at one time.

19.(a) Haymarket, looking north   Post 1895

This was the area where many of the North-east farmers came to sell their produce. The Farmer's Rest pub, which is still standing today, can be seen on the right of the photograph.

(b) 1993

The Haymarket is now dominated by a bus station and a taxi rank. The large structure at the extreme right is one of the multi-storey car parks in the Eldon Square Shopping Centre.

20.(a) Morpeth Castle Pub 1910

Our first stop for refreshment is at the Morpeth Castle public house on the corner of Percy Street and Leazes Lane. It is said that the beer was drawn from wooden barrels slung from a gantry as the pub did not have a cellar.

(b) 1993

Sorry to whet your appetite, the pub is now a furniture shop.

21. (a) Bourgognes Pub 1966

This building was originally the town jailer's house at 146 Newgate Street and was built in 1634. It became a public house under the name of The Mason's Arms before the well known name of Bourgognes. Sadly it was demolished in 1972.

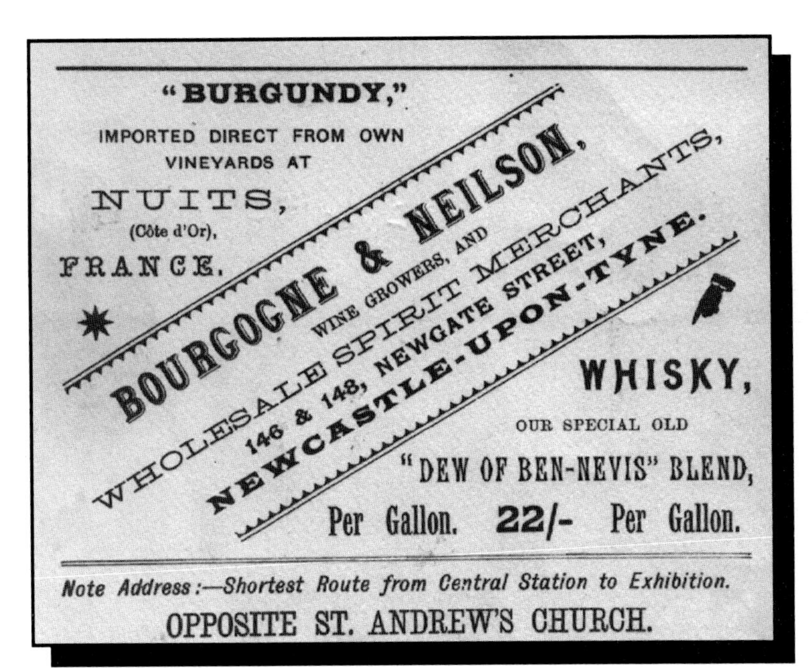

(b) 1887

Whisky is only 14p per pint at Bourgognes.

(c) 1993

Bourgognes re-appeared a few years later further down the road as part of the Eldon Square complex

22. (a) Gallowgate 1890

As the name suggests Gallowgate was a gate in the town wall which led to the gallows which were on the town moor. The hoardings on the shop at the right are advertising Dewar's whisky and Sunlight soap. The building with the wood panel frontage is the premises of Duncan & Daglish Ltd; importers and bonders.

(b) 1993

None of the original buildings has survived and Gallowgate is better known by Newcastle United fans as a road which leads to St James' Park football ground and not to the gallows.

23. (a) Gallowgate 2 c1890

This is a view of the opposite side of the street to the previous shot. It shows the premises of Carver & Co a furniture depository business. Carver also had premises in the Royal Arcade on Pilgrim Street. Strawberry Lane is seen on the left of the picture.

(b) 1960's

This view shows the public baths which were where Tynesider's of the 19th Century went to get clean, not to swim and enjoy themselves.

(c) 1993

Sadly the baths have gone and nothing has been built to replace them.

BYKER

Byker is a suburb of Newcastle to the east of the City. The name Byker means *by kiarr*; neighbouring upon a marsh. Byker flourished in the 1870's when hundreds of flats were built to accommodate the industrial workers in the area.

24.(a) Byker Tavern, Byker Bank 1920

Byker Tavern was at No 70 Byker Bank at the junction with Dunn Place which is seen on the left. The Byker Tavern was one of about five pubs on Byker Bank in 1910. The pub was closed in 1970.

(b) 1970

The surrounding buildings have been demolished in preparation for the building of new housing as part of the Byker Wall complex.

(c) 1993

The pub was demolished soon after the above photograph. The new housing now extends from Byker Bank east to Union Road.

25.(a) The Blue Bell Pub, Shields Road 1910

The Blue Bell pub was built around 1770. The chimney of Newcastle Corporation's refuse destructor can be seen on the left of the photograph. A slaughterhouse was situated at the end of the terrace houses to the right of the Blue Bell.

(b) 1953

This is the same view 43 years later. The Blue Bell has lost its fairy-tale castle spires. The Black's Regal cinema can just be seen behind the extreme left hand lamp-post. It was built in 1934 and was a popular cinema for over two decades.

(c) 1993

The Black's Regal cinema was eventually demolished after serving as a bingo hall for a while, however the Blue Bell continues to do business.

26. (a) Byker Square 1897

Again the Blue Bell pub can be seen in the centre. The very old house to the left of the Blue Bell is one of the Byker Square dwellings.

(b) 1993

The Blue Bell and Lord Clyde pubs are still serving pints as is the Byker & Heaton Union Club in the distance.

27. (a) Byker Hill

This is the stretch of Shields Road between Byker Square and Chillingham Road. The Sun picture house was situated to the right of the photograph.

(b) 1960's

This photograph is actually from the 1960's however little has changed in the main view. The houses on the right however have been demolished. The view shows the East-End Clinic where many young Geordie lads and lasses got their polio "jabs".

28. (a) North View School, Brough Street. 1966

This fine school was built in Victorian times and featured separate playgrounds for the boys and girls. In class however, each boy was made to sit next to a girl as the author can confirm as North View School is where he received his primary education.

(b) 1993

Brough Street is still there in name, however North View School has been demolished and replaced by Northfields House, being sheltered accommodation for old people. The rows of terraced houses have been replaced by very pleasant new dwellings. The bell tower from the school is now at Beamish museum.

29. (a) Steam Bus at Byker Car Sheds c1917

This fine example of British engineering was built by a company called Sentinel. Newcastle Corporation transport, garaged many of its buses and trams at Byker car sheds which were (and still are) on Shields Road just east of the junction with Chillingham Road.

(b) Byker Transport Depot 1993

This modern minibus gives the commuters a more comfortable ride than the old steam bus.

30. (a) Shields Road (east) 1901

This is looking east towards C.A. Parsons steam turbine works at what must have been a shift change time. The works can just be seen through the mist at the end of the row of terraced flats. Henley Street is on the left. Chapman Street ran parallel to Shields Road behind the terraced houses in this picture. The street was named after Chapman, the inventor of a coal-hauling device called the Chain-Eater.

(b) 1990

The rows of terraced flats have long since disappeared giving a clear view of Parsons main office block; Parsons is now part of the NEI- Rolls Royce group of companies. Further down Shields Road on the right was the Author's childhood home; No. 516 Shields Road.

31. (a) Tram on Chillingham Road 1948

The No 17 class "E" tram to Heworth crosses the Coast Road long before the Motorway to Tynemouth was constructed.

(b) 1993

The Coast Road motorway now passes underneath the round-a-bout at this intersection with Chillingham Road/Benton Road and diesel -engine buses now operate the routes.

32. (a) Benton Four Lane Ends

Traders in their horses and carts go about their business on Front Street leading to Whitley Road on a cold winter's day.

(b) 1991

The old farmhouse has been renovated and is now part of the Teal Close Nomad Housing development. Four Lane Ends is now the site of an interchange between omnibuses and Metro trains in Newcastle's public transport network.

FOREST HALL

33. (a) Forest Hall Village c 1910

Up till the early 1960's, Forest Hall was a quiet village situated to the north-east of Newcastle. Never-the-less Forest Hall had a railway station which was on the main line from Newcastle to Edinburgh and the photograph shows the station's signal box which overlooked the level crossing.

(b) 1993

In 1964 a flyover was built over the railway line which made the level crossing redundant. The terraced shops on the left were demolished to make way for a new shopping centre which is when Forest Hall ceased to be a quiet village.

34. (a) Clousden Hill Pub, Forest Hall c. 1900

This is at the north end of Forest Hall at the junction of Forest Hall Road and Great Lime Road. The author's father, Jack Phillips, found the old horse trough rusting away in a council yard in Springfield Park, Forest Hall and in 1974 he talked the council into erecting the trough quite close to its original site.

(b) 1974

Jack Phillips proudly exhibits the re-conditioned horse trough which was shown in the early photograph at the turn of the century. Jack suggested that the trough should be re-sited at the same spot and used at the centre of a mini round-a-bout.

(c) 1993

The horse trough now functions as a flower pot. The Clousden Hill Inn is still in business but has changed its name to the Tut 'n' Shive.

35. (a) Wheatsheaf Pub, New York 1926

In 1926, the camera was still a curiosity; enough to get Tyneside drinking men to leave their beers on the counter for a few minutes to have their photographs taken. Children and livestock were also displayed for the cameraman.

(b) 1993

The Wheatsheaf, The Dun Cow and the Robin Hood Inn are all very interesting old pubs within walking distance of each other in New York; a small village about 2 miles west of Whitley Bay.

36. (a) Cannon Inn, Earsdon c1925

Patrons of the Cannon Inn sit four abreast in Mr Wakefield's charabanc ready to set off for a day trip, to the races? Wherever they are going, they are not going to get there very fast as the bus's speed is limited to 12 miles per hour.

(b) 1967

Earsdon is unspoilt by progress and remains a beautiful Tyneside village isolated from the main traffic by a bypass.

37. (a) Bee Hive, Earsdon

The Bee Hive pub has changed very little in over 250 years since it was first built. Even in the 1960's it did not have a mains electricity supply and relied on a diesel generator for its power.

(b) 1993

The Bee Hive is known and loved by countless pub go-ers from all over Tyneside and is very popular during the summer months. It is located on the narrow twisting road from Earsdon to Old Hartley; a road which is reported to be used by some drivers to test the performance of car and driver.

38. (a) Old Hartley, West End 1906

Old Hartley was a small colliery village just 1/2 mile south of Seaton Sluice and this 1906 photograph shows the row of miner's cottages on the bank leading to the cross roads with the road from Seaton Sluice to Whitley Bay. On the right is Pake's shop. In the 1850's a terrible mining disaster resulted in the death of over 200 men and boys.

(b) 1993

To the right is the road to Seaton Sluice and further right, off camera, is the very historic pub, The Deleval Arms Hotel. On a clear day there is a beautiful view of Whitley Bay and the Spanish City from this spot.

WHITLEY BAY
39.(a) St Mary's Island 1890

Before the lighthouse was built it was recorded that mariners were warned and guided by the light which burned in the sanctuary of the little chapel on the island. The name St Mary's Island comes from the tradition of the sea where such guiding lights were known as "our Lady's light".

(b) 1896

This view shows the lighthouse under construction.

(c) 1993

The lighthouse is no longer in service as an aid to navigation but now houses a museum.

40. (a) The Three Ships, Whitley Bay 1900

This view is at the south end of Park Avenue and shows the first Ship Inn as a simple whitewash-walled building. St Paul's Church is seen in the centre.

(b) 1920's

The single storey building has now been replaced by the New Ship Hotel being a fine brick structure. The 1920's photographer has entered into the spirit of Tyneside: Past & Present by lining up the church roof crosses exactly like the 1900 shot.

(c) 1991

St Paul's church still remains but a third Ship Hotel has been built in the same spot. The 1990's photographer risked life and limb standing in the middle of the road to get the same camera angle.

41. (a) The Old Post Office, Whitley Bay

This very early photograph of Whitley Bay shows the old post office on Front Street.

(b) 1993

The Victoria pub is still standing and has been a very popular pub for many years.

CULLERCOATS

42. (a) Flood at Cullercoats Station 1900

It was October 1900 when heavy rainfall caused severe flooding at Cullercoats station. The village's fishermen were called upon to launch their boats from the platform to rescue passengers from the stranded train.

(b) Metro Train 1993

The station is now part of the Tyneside Metro Rapid Transit system.

43. (a) Tynemouth Front Street 1848

This fascinating view shows the style of dress the men and women wore in 1848.

(b) Title

Many of the houses are still present but you have to look very carefully to match them from the old to the new view.

44. (a) The Foxhunter's Inn, Preston Village 1920

Many Geordie's will know the Foxhunter's Inn as a posh public house and restaurant in Prestongate near Whitley Bay but who would have thought it started trading at these premises just down the road in Preston village.

(b) 1993

The Foxhunter's Inn is now situated in Prestongate near the Preston Grange Estate and this building is now a "tuck" shop. To the right, just out of camera is Preston Cottage and behind the cameraman is Tyneside Pool swimming baths.

45.(a) Opening of the Coast Road 1927

The new road from Newcastle to Shields which bypassed Wallsend was welcomed by the residents of Wallsend, whose high street was the on the mains route for the fish carts from North Shields to the City.

(b) Coast Road 1993

The Coast Road was widened to a three lane express route in the 1960's and now carries a lot more traffic than fish-carts. The cigarette factory of W.D. & H.O. Wills can be seen behind the bridge, however cigarette production ceased there several years ago.

46. (a) West Road, Denton Burn

This is a view of the West Road looking west. The road followed the course of the Roman Wall.

(b) 1991

Further west, the road widens to a dual carriageway which continues through to Hexham.

47. (a) Tram at Lemington

A tram from Newcastle is seen passing through a cutting into Lemington village which is west of Newcastle on the banks of the River Tyne.

(b) 1991

The tramline has been replaced by a bypass however the very interesting pub called the New Tyne Iron remains intact.

The Links Between the Photographs

For the benefit of those readers who have not been able to identify the links between the old views and the new, here is a list. The more obvious links are not included. If there is no link then it is stated so, to put the reader out of their misery.

2. **The Guildhall, Quayside**
   No link.
3. **Quayside**
   No link
5. **First Electric Train**
   No link.
6. **Collingwood Street**
   The building to the right of Pape's building. Notice an extra storey has been added.
8. **Pudding Chare**
   The iron post at the bottom left of the picture.
9. **Pudding Chare 2**
   The type foundry in the foreground. Notice the iron post is there also in the distance.
12. **Northumberland Street**
    Amos Atkinson's two storey shop on the right.
14. **Fenwick's, Northumberland Street**
    No 41 Northumberland Street; now a bookshop.
15. **Haymarket**
    Notice the Newcastle Brewery's building on the right is also unchanged as well as the war memorial.
16. **The Hancock Museum.**
    The Museum itself.
17. **The North-East Coast Exhibition**
    The Palace of Arts building with the round dome.
18. **Percy Street**
    Bruce's Building window on the left.
19. **Haymarket**
    St Thomas' Church in the distance, Farmers Rest pub on the right and the building which is now a travel agent on the right.
20. **Morpeth Castle Pub**
    The wall of the building slopes outover.

21. **Bourgognes Pub**
No link
22. **Gallowgate**
No link
23. **Gallowgate 2**
No link between a) and b) and St Andrew's House wall on the right between b) and c).
24. **Byker Tavern**
The links between 1970 and 1993 are the buildings in the distance on the right.
25. **Blue Bell Pub, Byker**
Notice that the buildings on the left and right are the same.
26. **Byker Hill**
As well at the Blue Bell pub, the Lord Clyde pub and what is now Byker & Heaton Union Club.
27. **Shields Road**
No link
28. **North View School, Byker**
The terraced houses in the distance across the railway cutting.
29. **Byker Car Sheds**
No link, but notice the ventilation louvers in the roof in the old photograph and a similar structure has been roof-felted over in the 1993 photograph.
30. **Shields Road, Parsons**
No major link, but the gable end of the old offices of Parsons as shown on the new photograph tie in with the offices barely visible through the mist in the old shot.
31. **Tram on Chillingham Road**
The Tudor style buildings at the left.
32. **Four Lane Ends**
The farmhouse in the centre.
33. **Forest Hall Village**
The terraced buildings on the right, especially the attic windows.
38. **Old Hartley**
The old-fashioned sign-post (one of the vanes of the signpost has fallen off on the new photograph.)
41. **The Old Post Office, Whitley Bay**
The Victoria pub.

42. Flood at Cullercoats
The building at the top left also the wall with a notice at the end of the platform.

44. Foxhunter's Inn, Preston Village
Notice the attic windows on the house at the right.

45. Coast Road
The bridge.

46. West Road
No link

47. Tram at Lemington.
The New Tyne Iron pub and the houses on the left.

Acknowledgements

The author would like to thank Craig Oliphant for taking the new photographs and printing some of the very old negatives of the early views. Thanks also go to the staff of Newcastle Central Library Local Studies Department for their help in the research work and thank you to Horsley Hall for checking the script. Finally, thank you to my wife June for tolerating me throughout the project.